AN INTRODUCTION

TO THE CHRISTIAN FAITH

ROOTS
and
FRUIT

Timothy E.G. Bartel

CALLA PRESS
PUBLISHING

CONTENTS

"O thou lord of life, send my roots rain"

—*Gerard Manley Hopkins,*

"Thou art indeed just, Lord"

From the earliest centuries of the church, Christians have written poems that introduce and summarize their beliefs. This book continues that tradition for the 21st century. *Roots and Fruit* is an introduction to Christianity for anyone who wonders what it's all about. What do Christians believe? Who are their heroes? Why do they do things like get baptized, or talk about resurrection? This book is an introduction to the *why* of these things. In these pages, the reader will encounter the most important stories from the Bible: God's creation of the world; the fall of humanity; God's salvation of the people of Israel from slavery in Egypt; the life, death, and resurrection of Jesus, and more. In these stories we meet great heroes and heroines of the Christian faith: Rachel, Joseph, Moses, Mary, John, and others. Paralleling the biblical stories are explanations of how these stories form the beliefs and practices of Christians, from the doctrines of the Trinity and the incarnation to practices like prayer and communion.

Roots and Fruit is written in poetic verse. As someone trained in both theology and poetry, I wanted to offer readers an introduction to Christianity that was a little different from anything else out there. Short poems can be inviting in ways that long passages of prose are not, and I love how the beauty of a poem's rhythm can help to highlight the power of its subject. Christians have traditionally cared deeply for beauty: I believe now more than ever we need to recover the connection between the beauty of the natural world and the ultimate meaning of our lives.

One more note: *Roots and Fruit* is only an introduction to the Christian Faith, and is not meant to be an exhaustive explanation of the biblical narrative or Christian theology. For those who wish to learn more about the Bible or the teachings of the Christian church, each narrative poem includes footnotes referencing the books and chapters of the Bible that each poem references and retells. If nothing else, *Roots and Fruit* is an invitation to read the Bible, whether it's your first time or your fifty-first. There are suggestions for further reading at the back of the book.

Prologue: Spring

Old oaks are thriving in the humid air.
Below, in what is left of prairie grass,
The acorns that took root last autumn now
Are shooting up new oaks into the world.

Some surely will be drowned in summer rain,
And more will last to die in winter freezes,
But just a few will weather wet and ice
With deep determined roots, and—with the grace

Of nature's nourishment—they will grow tall,
Will welcome each new spring with stretching boughs
As if they could embrace the aging world.

BOOK I

Life

Begin with life, the life of girls and trees
And hawks and galaxies—these lives appear
To us as precious—no one needs to be
Convinced these things are lovely. We are born

Enamored with the given world; we love
Exorbitantly naturally. A boy
Will love each sticky snail, will hoard each rock
He finds as if it were a treasure rare

And worthy of defense. Begin with life,
Not just the lives we treasure, but the lives
That treasure all the objects of the world.
This life, these loves, they have a ground, a source.

The Source

No one has ever seen the source of life,
Nor could it be a thing we see or touch.
The source and sustenance of life would be
A higher, wiser being than the life

It makes. And yet intention, purpose, plan
Seem evident in how the lives and loves
Appear and intermingle in the world.
A woman will encounter, once, a grove

In which a peace inheres, and she will come
Into that grove to find a silence that
She cannot find another place—but there
The loveliness of oaks is wound around

A mystery of meaning. She will sit,
Discern a solid center to the world.

Theology I

We think and speak of God in words, but know
That God—*Deus, Theos, Allah*—is past
All language. Still, He meets us in the realm
Of speech and gives coherent words to say

So we might reach our minds toward Him and
        glimpse
Beyond and through the syllables and sounds
A blossoming reality that is
The substance that the language images—

Just as an artist will devote his life
To getting all the lines and shadings right
But never will mistake them for his wife.

Theology II

We say that God is one, and there are none
Like God. And he is Person, not just Force
Or Law. But though we call Him *God*,
And *Him*, and say His holy name *I am*,

We cannot know Him in His essence, for
Our God is not a man, nor concept, nor
Is He like any thing that has been made.
Beyond, before, beneath, between—beyond

The world and stars, beyond all being: there
You'll find *I am*, beyond all we believe
And disbelief, beyond all knowing and
All ignorance. And He is never lonely.

The Sage[1]

A Hebrew sage named Moses wrote a book
(Three thousand years ago and more), about
The source of life. He said the source did not
Have any name but this: *I am*. He told

His readers of the making of the world,
How this *I am* brought forth the universe
By power of His Word and brooding of
His Spirit. First God said: let there be light,

Time, day, night, stars, moon, oak, the homing bat,
Titanic whale, the warm and watered soil,
This middle earth, where we live out our loves.

---

[1] Genesis 1.

Trinity

We say that God is one in nature: one
Divine and supernatural being, and
We say that He exists as persons: three
Distinct and holy persons: Father, Son,

And Spirit, a relationship of love
Within the heart of everything. The Son
Was there in the beginning with the Father.
He is the Father's Word by which all things

Were made. He is the one begotten Son.
The Spirit, who proceeds from Father, was
With them as well in that beginning, when
He brooded on each fructifying world.

The Garden[2]

Imagine, Moses says, a garden in
The dawning of the world. And there *I am*
Makes humans, man and woman, like Himself.
Like Him they are creative and like Him

They think, and name, and love created things.
But unlike Him they are composed of dust,
And will return to dust if they do not
Remain connected to their lasting source.

I am makes friends of them, tells them to be
Like blooming things: "Be fruitful, bear more life,
But do not seek what you're not ready for."

---

[2] Genesis 2.

Creation

We say that God created out of nothing;
No matter was—not even chaos—there
Before He spoke the universe to life.
All things material and spiritual,

Each object, every soul, was made by God.
They did not emanate from Him as if
They shared His nature. He surpasses all—
God wholly uncreated, world created,

And if created, then created well.
All matter, spirit, soul is very good,
For God has loved the world since the beginning,
And all created things have lasting worth.

Cosmos

We say because the universe was made
By God, there is intention in each thing—
From plankton, plant, and person to the vast
Array of planets, quasars, stars, there is

A meaning and an order to them all.
There is a meaning to the arc of comets,
A meaning to migration in the spring,
For God delights to hide a purpose deep,

Delights to see our stunned discovering.

The Tree[3]

There was a tree—imagine it—within
The garden. It was not for humans, yet.
I am explained this: "Do not eat from it,
For if you do then death will come to you."

But they were tempted (who would tempt these two?)
And they—the woman, then the man—they *ate.*
Then death, it crept into the world, into
Their chests, their heads. They bargained and they
        blamed,

But wise *I am* expelled them from the garden,
And placed a fatal guard before its gates.

---

[3] Genesis 3.

God's Image

We say that man and woman—humankind—
Were made according to God's image, and
His likeness is a thing that humans share
Uniquely with him. Likeness unto God

Is found in virtue: faith and hope and love
(Love most of all, a love that bears all fruit).
And reason and creative making are
A part of God's own image. But our will

Which also is like God's own will, is free
To choose these virtues or reject them. So,
When man and woman disobeyed *I am*,
They stepped away toward nothingness, toward death.

The Tempter

But who would tempt these two? A serpent, but
No ordinary snake, instead it was
A spirit made both by and for *I am*
But free to choose—it chose itself instead.

It told the woman she would be as wise
As wise *I am* if she would eat the fruit
From that forbidden tree. The woman chose
To eat and see; the man with her ate, too.

Their exile came with curses from *I am*:
The man would work the earth to bear him food,
And woman too would labor, bearing men.

Angels

There are more things in earth and heaven than
Are dreamed in man's philosophies. We say
That God created other spirits in
The world's beginning: angels, meant to have

No earthly bodies—subtle minds are theirs,
And flashing intellects beyond our own.
In thousands they await *I am*'s decrees
And speed to carry out His vast designs.

But one, the tempter, chose himself instead
Of God's directives. Satan was his name,
Who drew a thousand demons to his cause,
Then turned his eyes toward men, to make them fall.

History Begins[4]

Come see the humans rise: the men who kill,
The men who build hard cities up, the men
Who boast and innovate. See women, too,
Who learn to make their will through trick and grit

And hope and sisterhood where men have failed.
But some remember that their father and
Their mother once were friends with God. Those who
Remember this begin to call on Him.

He answers in the stars and in the dew.
He calls them out from violence and pride
Into the promise of His friendship still.

---

[4] Genesis 4–5.

Abraham[5]

A man and woman, Abraham and Sarah,
Were two who left their homes to follow God
Into a wilderness, seeking a land
I am had promised them. "Come see the stars,"

I am once said to Abraham. The night
Was filled with pricks of light beyond his counting.
"This is what your descendants will be like
If you will follow me." So Abraham

Believed the words of God, and he was called
A man of righteousness for his belief.

---

[5] Genesis 12, 13, 15.

The Chosen People

We say that God is one who chooses some
To be His own: He calls just Abraham
And no one else around him. And he shows
To Abraham His plan: a people will

Arise from his descendants who will be
A nation dedicated to *I am*
Who dwell in places God has chosen and
Who follow laws that God has made. A light

To other nations they will be, a guide
To how all people may raise boughs and thrive.

Sons of Abraham[6]

A line of lovers sprang from Abraham,
A line of men who wrestled with themselves,
With one another, and—at last—with God,
With God, who works His will through mortal lives.

First, Isaac came, who married fair Rebecca;
They waited for, begot two wrestling twins:
The older, Esau, dark of hair and strong,
And wiry Jacob, full of tricks and game

For all adventures time might throw his way.

---

[6] Genesis 32, 35.

Adventures[7]

Imagine the adventurer: from birth
He wrestled with his brother Esau for
The birthright of his father Isaac; masks
And double deals he mastered, how to hoax

A man to trade his fortune for a song,
And coax a feeble sheep to bear rich rams.
He slept on stones and woke to angel's wings,
Raised lonely altars in the wilderness.

One night, while journeying, he met *I am*
Beside a river; there they wrestled well,
And God was pinned by man; so in return
I am presented Jacob a new name.

---

[7] Genesis 25–28, 32.

Israel[8]

We say that man should wrestle with his God,
Should reckon, reason, reach, and grasp upon
The truth he finds within the wrestling.
For *Israel* means *one who strives with God.*

This is the name *I am* gave Jacob then,
And this is what is promised in that name:
That he who finds, through striving, God's deep truth,
Is gifted with what Jacob too beheld:

A ladder into heaven, where the bright
And lovely angels, holy, whole, ascend.
What holds you, then, from climbing up to God?

---

[8] Genesis 28, 32.

Two Wives[9]

Now Jacob was a lover like his father,
And travelled north to find a wife: he met
Young Rachel, Laban's daughter, by a well,
And providence played out a song of love.

For seven years he labored to win Rachel
But Laban tricked him, gave him Leah—so
For seven years again he worked to win
His Rachel and at last received his bride.

And Leah, dedicated to her work,
But less beloved, bore ten mighty sons.
To Rachel two alone were born, both boys,
And Jacob loved her quietude and grace.

---

[9] Genesis 29.

Leah and Rachel

We say that Jacob's wives are images
Of two approaches we might take to life.
First, Leah is the way of action, where
Our time is spent in useful labor: works

Of service, giving alms, and tending to
The physical demands of life: food, fuel,
And clothing that we all must have to live.
There's worth in both the worker and the work.

And Rachel is the life of contemplation:
The body still and silent, now the mind
Begins to search the realm of being for
The truth of things and—past all things—their source.

Joseph[10]

Of Rachel's sons, young Joseph was the one
Who pleased his aging father most; he smiled
And glistened with the gifts of Israel.
How his eleven brothers envied him!

They plotted, sold him into slavery.
In Egypt, exiled, Joseph found himself
The servant of the noble Potiphar,
Whose lovely wife desired him like wine.

Invited to her bed, young Joseph feared
I am and fled from her temptations. Hurt,
She spread the lie that Joseph had attacked her.
And Joseph, twice betrayed, was thrown in prison.

---

[10] Genesis 37, 39.

Chastity

We say that God made humans to enjoy
In moderation all the pleasures of
The body: food and drink and also sex.
There is a joy and mystery in how

A woman and a man unite, grow roots
And blossom into fruitfulness. Because
Of this, we say that marriage is a state
Of holy union, not to be betrayed

By either spouse uniting with another.
And Joseph is our model in this art:
To flee adultery, to honor marriage,
And keep our wills controlled by mind, not lust.

Egypt[11]

I am remained with Joseph in the land
Of Egypt, raised him up from slave to lord
Of all of Egypt. For the Pharaoh found
The prisoner Joseph could interpret dreams

And wielded wisdom far beyond all others.
Then Joseph's wisdom, granted by *I am*,
Saved all who lived in Egypt and around it:
A famine struck the land, but Joseph had

Foreseen it in a dream. He stored up food
For all who needed it. Soon Israel
Sent sons to Egypt, begging for some bread—

---

[11] Genesis 40–42.

Brothers[12]

Imagine this: eleven brothers come
From little towns to Egypt, realm of kings,
To buy some grain—to live another year,
And keep their aging father fed in grief.

They meet a man who might as well be king,
He glistens so with gifts from Pharaoh's bounty.
He calls them spies; he sells them grain; he gives
Their money back; he turns and names them thieves.

And finally, to their bewildered eyes,
He cries: "See! I am Joseph! No, don't fear.
Our God has worked all things unto our good.
Send for our father; you will live with me."

---

[12] Genesis 42–46.

Providence

We say that God allowed both slavery
And slander to afflict the righteous Joseph
Not so he may be hurt, but so that he
Might find himself the savior of the land

Of Egypt in the coming famine. God
Works through the mess of history that man
Has made, and leads His people to the place
He has prepared for them, past sin, past pain.

This providence of God outstrips our minds
And those who try to guess God's plan prove fools.

Slavery[13]

Four hundred years the sons of Israel
Lived in the land of Egypt. Over time
The deeds of Joseph were forgotten and
New Pharaohs feared and hated those twelve tribes.

Then slavery was all that Israel
Began to know, and male children born
To Israel were killed by Pharaoh's soldiers—
But one wise woman saved her newborn son,

Put him into a basket on the Nile,
Where he escaped the swords and drifted to
The palace of the Pharaoh. There he lived,
There grew, grew strong—and Moses was his name.

---

[13] Exodus 1–2.

Moses[14]

Yes, Moses, you already know his work.
His story is the most important, save
The story of the Christ. For Moses found
Himself a prince of Egypt and a kin

To Egypt's slaves. When he was grown, he fled
Into the desert, tended sheep, took time
Away from the complexities he faced.
One day he found a wonder in the hills:

A burning bush that would not fall to ash,
But kept its bloom within the crucible.
And out of it a voice: "I am *I am*
And I have come to set My people free."

---

[14] Exodus 2–3.

Aflame but Unconsumed

We say that Moses met within the bush
I am Himself. As flames in branches, God
At times may rest within created things,
And not consume them. Humans too may make

Themselves into the kind of beings God
Can dwell within—a purity of heart,
Obedience to God, and active love
Are what prepare a human to receive

God's flame of grace. And such was Moses, who
Would speak to God as to a friend, whose face
Once shone as bright as sunlight on the mountain.

Out of Egypt[15]

Reluctant but emboldened by his God,
The exiled Moses entered Egypt to
Demand from Pharaoh freedom for his race.
The king refused, and God sent plague and storm,

And death to Egypt. But the Israelites
Were spared these plagues, for God commanded them
To paint a stipe of blood upon the doorways
Of every faithful house, then eat the lambs

From which the blood was spilled. They heard the
            cries
That rose from Egypt, cries of grief, remorse.
Then Pharaoh cast the tribes of Israel
Into the desert. Moses guided them.

---

[15] Exodus 7–13.

The Sea, The Sea[16]

The hosts of Israel, grown strong and lean
Beneath the whips of Egypt, flooded out
From slavery. The sea was in their way—
The red sea, hemming them from freedom. Soon

The Pharaoh changed his mind and mustered men
To hunt the Israelites and bring them back
To bondage. Caught between the water and
The chariots of Pharoah, Moses called

His people to have faith—God would not rest
From wonders. Then the waters rose and gaped
And Israel walked through on solid ground.
Then high waves turned and drowned the Pharoah's
	hosts.

---

[16] Exodus 14.

Freedom

We say *I am* has set the captives free.
He heard His people groaning in the night
Of servitude, where Egypt kept their necks
Bent down to mud: no hope, no promised land

Was in their minds. But God despises those
Who treat their fellow humans not like free
And equal beings, but like beasts to bear
Unjust demands and burdens. God defies

The slaver and the kidnapper and those
Who benefit from all their wicked work.

The Law[17]

I am showed miracles can happen in
Even the desert places: food and drink,
Deliverance from enemies, and more.
For God met Moses and his people on

The mount called Sinai, and He wrote his Law
For them upon the very stones: how they
Should live, should organize community
Around both purity and justice for

Their health and their endurance through the dark
Of history, still cursed from that first fall.
The center of the Law was blood, blood drawn
From spotless lambs and offered by pure priests.

---

[17] Exodus 14–20.

The First Commandment[18]

Imagine, now, the mountain of the Lord,
Where cloud and thunder cluster: there within
The cloud the prophet Moses speaks with God
As you speak face to face with friend or lover.

Commandments, ten of them, are at the heart
Of all the Law *I am* reveals, ten guides
To shape a life—to shape a nation too.
The first is this: that we should have no gods

Before *I am*. He is Source of all,
Who brought His people out of slavery,
And He alone is worthy of our worship.

---

[18] Exodus 19–20.

The Second Commandment[19]

Commandment two: to shape no idol from
The clay, or wood, or gold, to never bow
To graven gods like other nations do.
I am alone is worthy; who is Zeus

Or Baal or Jupiter before *I am*?
If they exist at all, they live through Him.
A shining calf of gold—is this your god?
Is this the one who raised you from the pit?

Before, beyond, beneath *I am* abides,
And all attempts to make a shape divine
Will crumble set before His majesty.

---

[19] Exodus 20, 32.

The Third Commandment[20]

I am is holy even in His name,
To speak the name of God requires respect
And reverence. The third command is this:
Do not take God's own name in vain.

And what is vanity? The word unmeant,
The word flung out in bitter flippancy,
The craven act of saying: "Thus says God,"
And then pronouncing only our own whims.

Fall down, oh princes, at the name of God,
And bow, all mighty men, at His commands;
Throw wide the golden gates, for He draws near.

---

[20] Exodus 20, Psalm 24.

The Fourth Commandment[21]

Our hearts are restless; roaming earth and thought
We wander and we work, but seek an end
Beyond our work—a holiday, a Sabbath.
This is the fourth commandment: each new week

Observe a day of rest and honor it.
Man was not made for work, but work for man,
And God, who never tires, when He had framed
The universe in six successive days

Sat down the seventh day and rested well.
So keep the seventh day a day of rest—rest, rich and
     poor;
Rest, young and old; rest, immigrants and servants.
Let life on earth taste rest and live in hope.

---

[21] Exodus 20, 31.

The Fifth Commandment[22]

Back in the garden God told man and woman,
"Be fruitful; multiply and fill the Earth,"
And those in every age who keep His word
Establish families of children. Thus

The fifth commandment: Honor both your parents,
And you will prosper in the land. Do not
Regard them as your enemies or take
Advantage of their generosity.

There was a man who took his father's wealth
And wasted it within a foreign land;
Remorseful he returned, expecting judgement,
But found forgiveness in his father's arms.

---

[22] Genesis 1, Exodus 20, Luke 15.

The Sixth Commandment[23]

Begin with life: the life of human selves,
Who worship, labor, rest, and honor—selves
Created and at last returned to God,
Who treasures every human life and love.

This is the sixth commandment: do not kill.
If someone sheds another's blood, the blood
Of he who murdered will be owed to God.
What can you do, oh you who kill your brother?

Where can you run when blood itself cries out?
There is an altar on which human fault
May be laid down and expiated in
A purifying flame—make that your end.

---

[23] Genesis 9, Exodus 20, Leviticus 4.

The Seventh Commandment[24]

Let love be strong as death; let marriages
Be sites of growing strength and spreading boughs;
Let every lover set a lover's seal
Upon their lips, upon their inmost heart,

To never give to strangers what is bound
Within the sacred seal of married love.
And so commandment seven says: do not
Commit adultery. Be governed as

Young Joseph was, who fled adultery,
But, when the time was right, awakened love
With Asenath—they blossomed, bearing sons.

---

[24] Song of Songs 8, Exodus 20, Genesis 41.

The Eighth Commandment[25]

If life is precious, so is all God gives
To each and every human: homes and hearths,
The field we sow, the harvest we collect,
The tools with which our daily work is done.

This is the eighth commandment: do not steal.
The land your neighbor has, let it be hers,
For every worker's worthy of the wage
They earn. The wise investor's worthy too.

Instead of taking, give. The giving act
Undoes the sin of theft, restores the land.

---

[25] Exodus 20, 1 Timothy 5.

The Ninth Commandment[26]

A principle is active in these last
Commandments: that the honest act is best.
And now we come to words. This is the ninth
Commandment: do not give a false account—

Whether in court, condemning guiltless men,
Or in the privacy of daily life.
Let every word be true and in accord
With how the world is—not how you wish.

I am is Lord of Truth: He made all things,
And binds together even sound and sense.
Oh, what a piece of work is man, that he
Would wrench his words from what they should have
  meant.

---

[26] Exodus 20.

The Tenth Commandment[27]

Your subtle acts are open to *I am.*
He sees beyond the veil of skin and smile
Into the heart, into the inmost thought,
And asks for justice and for truth within.

This is the tenth commandment: do not covet.
From coveting springs forth a host of faults,
Springs murder, theft, adultery, deceit.
The roving eye of man alights upon

The prize of someone else; he yearns for it,
And plots and plots, and poisons his soft heart.
What would a nation of such men be like?
What light could shine from those who practiced
        justice?

---

[27] Exodus 20, Isaiah 58.

Promises and Kings[28]

The Law became the guide of Israel
Through deserts into Canaan, land of promise.
And many wars were waged there to establish
The tribes within the land—oh, they forgot

So many times *I am* and worshiped gods
Of other peoples, who were cruel and led
The sons of Israel into injustice,
Forgetting both the Law and how they had

Been saved by God to be no longer slaves.
Then kings arose among the Israelites,
And splintered those twelve tribes in half through
      war.

---

[28] Joshua, Judges, Samuel, Kings.

Prophecies[29]

We say that even in their wickedness
I am did not abandon Israel
But sent them prophets, men who spoke the words
Of God in warning and in comfort too.

One prophet's words spoke of a miracle:
A child was coming called Emmanuel,
Born from a virgin's womb, upon whose shoulders
The kingdoms of the aging earth would sit

And who would be a prince of peace. We say
This is the Christ, the promised one, who was
Announced through prophecy to Israel.

---

[29] Isaiah 9.

BOOK II

The Fullness of Time[30]

At times the rulers and at times the ruled,
The Israelites, the chosen of *I am*,
Reduced by war, captivity, and time
To Judah's tribe, called Jews, at last emerged

From history into the Pax Romana.
Then Rome was ruler of the promised land
And Jewish priests preserved Mosaic laws
Like fading paintings, almost lost to time.

From ranks of angels, one descended, found
A Jewish girl at her daily tasks.
He said: "Hail Mary, full of grace; *I am*
Has chosen you to bear His only Son."

---

[30] I Maccabees, Luke 1.

The Song of Mary

And Mary questioned this angelic one:
How could she bear when she was not yet married?
"The Holy Spirit will conceive the child
Within you—He will be the only One

Born of a virgin, child of God Himself."
Then Mary answered *yes*, and raised her voice
In song: "My soul, it magnifies *I am*,
For he will lift the lowly from the dust

"And cast the mighty from their palaces.
Now every generation will adore
My Son and call me blessed of womankind."

Bearer of God

We say that Mary is the mother of
Not just a man, but God Himself, for she
Knew from the very start her son would be
A savior for her people. All who speak

Of Mary speak of her with reverence,
For she is what we all must seek to be:
The one who answers *yes* to God, who bears
Their God into the darkness of the world.

When Mary said that all will call her blessed
She spoke of every generation—thus
We call her blessed. We pray to love like she.

Nativity[31]

One night the virgin Mary bore a son,
Surrounded by the animals within
A stable, for there was no room for her
Within the inns of little Bethlehem.

And Joseph, Mary's fiancé, was with her.
He held her son, agreed upon the name
The angel told to Mary: *Jesus*, one
Who saves His people from their ills and sins.

Away among the hills a band of shepherds
Were startled to behold an angel who
Announced to them the baby—so they hunted
And found the stable, worshipping the child.

---

[31] Luke 2.

Incarnation

We say that God the timeless, God who bides
Beyond the furthest being that we know,
United with our nature in her womb.
The second person of the Trinity

The Son divine, the Word of God, He was
A single person always, but within
The virgin He took on another nature:
Our own. He was not two new persons, nor

Was His divinity in essence changed.
He was and is both God and man—like us
In every way, both soul and body, so
He could redeem all features of ourselves.

Royalty[32]

Not shepherds only, but a group of lords
From Persia found the child too. They brought
Him gifts of gold and frankincense and myrrh.
For they had seen a star which they revered

As clear announcement that a newborn king
Was born in Bethlehem. Through sand and heat
They sought the king and spread the word of Him,
But not all kings were happy at the news.

King Herod, ruler of the Jews, sent out
His soldiers to discover this new king
And kill him long before He came of age.
But Joseph took the boy and fled from them.

---

[32] Matthew 2.

High and Low

We say the shepherds and the royalty
Both come to Christ to show us that He is
The savior of all types of men, not just
The wise, who read the stars, interpret signs,

And have the means to travel cross the world,
But also to the lowest workers who
Have nothing but the stars for roofs each night.
This baby is for both of them, for all.

We say as well that Jesus shows Himself
In both the natural order of the stars
As well as miracles—all points to Him.

Egypt, again[33]

In Egypt, Jesus grew with Mary and
His earthly father Joseph, who had saved
His strange new family from Herod's swords.
But Herod passed away, and Joseph brought

His family to Nazareth to live
As carpenters, pursuing common work.
But Mary knew her son was no-one common.
And Jesus grew in wisdom. Earth grew old;

Revival trickled into Israel;
New prophets preached; young zealots sharpened
        blades—
And many felt a revelation looming.

---

[33] Matthew 2.

Baptism[34]

There was a prophet sent from God named John,
Cousin to Jesus. John intoned against
The sins of Israel and called them to
Repent by washing in the Jordan river.

Then Jesus came to meet him in the stream
And asked to be baptized. Wise John discerned
His God was standing there before him and
Refused. But Jesus said that it was right

That John should wash Him in the river's flow.
When Jesus rose up from the water, words
Rang from the sky: "This is My only Son!"
The Spirit, like a holy dove, descended.

---

[34] Matthew 3, Luke 3.

Theophany

We say the dove descending onto Christ
While God the Father's voice rang over Him
Became a revelation to the world
That God is Trinity—begotten Son

Beloved by the Father; Spirit, third,
Proceeding from the Father, Three in One.
And John the Baptist acts as prophet, who,
In his baptizing Jesus, shows the people

That Christ is God and God is Trinity.
All those who would repent should follow Him.

The Wilderness[35]

When Jesus had been baptized, He sought prayer
And fasting in the wilderness alone.
The tempter sought Him there, hoping to match
The ruin that he made of those first humans

Within the garden. Jesus met him with
A wisdom and discernment matched by none.
By Moses' law and words of prophecy
He spurned the tempter's wiles. Then angels came,

Brought Jesus food and comfort past the fight.
Prepared for ministry, Christ came at last
And preached a liberation to the world:
Freedom for prisoners; for the blind, new sight.

---

[35] Luke 4.

Prayer

We say that those who follow God should seek
To talk to Him, to think of Him, to live
In constant consciousness that He is near,
Sustaining, guiding us. This consciousness

And conversation with our God is prayer.
We say that Jesus is our model of
How we should pray. Temptation, hunger, fear:
These will distract us, if they can, from prayer.

But prayer is companionship with God,
And He is there beside us in our trials;
He waits to minister to us when we
Remember at the last to turn to Him.

Ministry[36]

And what a freedom Jesus brought: the lame
Stood up at his command; the blind did see.
His hands healed withered arms and bleeding feet.
He gazed into a thousand faces like

His own and loved them, praised the faith He found
In them that God could still save men. Beyond
What Moses did, beyond the judges, kings,
And prophets of past history, He strove

Even with demons, cast them from their hosts
And comforted the liberated selves.

---

[36] Luke 8–9.

Liberation

We say that just as God set free the slaves
From Egypt, led them to the promised land,
Thus showing to the nations that He was
A God who liberates, a God who guides,

So Jesus liberated those He met
From sickness and impurity—from lives
That felt to those who lived them like a chain.
We say He came to set us free, both from

Our illness, hateful thoughts, unguided lives,
And from our greater masters: sin and death.

Stories[37]

He was no silent healer. Jesus told
The people stories: once a man went out
And found a pearl beneath the earth; he sold
All that he owned to buy the land that held it.

And once a son took his inheritance
And spent it far away from home in sin
Until he starved—then, desperate, he fled home,
Fell at his father's feet, and was received

As if he had been dead and lived again.
And once a sower sowed some seed—most died
On rocky ground or choked by weeds, but some
Grew in a thriving soil—deep roots, bright fruit.

---

[37] Luke 8, 14–16.

Interpretations

We say that Jesus' stories teach us of
His kingdom, which is human life made whole.
The pearl is God's own kingdom, which is worth
Our selling all we have to enter it.

The son is humankind, who wastes their share
Of dignity and honor far from God,
But can, repenting, hasten to the house
Of God, and will be welcomed back with love.

The seed is this good news of Jesus, which
Can be drowned out by worldly cares, but will,
If we receive it well, transform our lives.

Disciples[38]

They followed him, the women, children, men
Who marveled at his works, trusted his words
Pitched with authority and grace: "My kingdom
Is not an earthly kingdom where the strong

Out-master those who beg and need. No, blessed
Are poor and hungry souls; blessed, those who thirst
For righteousness." Twelve men left job and home,
For what He offered: Andrew, Peter, James,

John, Matthew, and a few more treasured men—
Including Judas, who loved silver most.

---

[38] Luke 6.

Enemies[39]

Of course, some hated Jesus for his works.
The priests and rulers, jealous of the look
The people gave Him, plotted how they could
Entrap Him in his words, or show that He

Was no true Jew, had broken Moses' law.
But some, like Nicodemus, came by night,
Unnoticed by the other priests, and asked
Jesus if He was truly who He seemed.

And Jesus told them God had sent his Son
To save the race of humans from their sins,
And men should love their enemies, love all.

---

[39] John 3, Luke 22.

Mount Tabor[40]

With Peter, James, and John, Jesus ascended
A mountain. And He was transformed before
Their eyes: His face and clothing shone with light
Much brighter than the sun—and next to Him

Two prophets from the ancient days appeared.
One looked like Moses brought to life again.
The shocked disciples stammered, but a voice
From heaven silenced them: "This is my Son

"In Whom I am well pleased. Listen to Him."
The echo faded, prophets faded, light
Again became the common light of day.

---

[40] Luke 9.

Transfiguration

We say that on Mount Tabor, Peter, James
And John saw Christ transfigured, shining with
The light of His divinity, which had
Been dimmed before so they could bear his presence.

And Moses and Elijah stand with Christ
To show that Jesus will fulfill the Law
And all the prophecies that have been made.
For Jesus is the culmination of

The world's desires: divinity united
With human nature, shining like the sun.

Supper[41]

But on the night He was to be betrayed
By Judas who loved silver, Jesus took
His followers into an upper room
And ate with them, and gave to them commands:

"Love one another. Do not be afraid.
Abide in me like grafted vines; I'll be
Your roots. Bear fruit. Now take and eat this bread:
It is my body, broken for you all.

"And drink this wine: it is my blood, poured out
For you and for the world. You eat this meal
Together, ever to remember me.
Tonight some will deny me. Pray with me."

---

[41] John 15, Luke 22.

Communion

We say it is a sacred mystery,
This supper that He gave them—bread and wine—
Which also were, He said, His body and
His blood. To eat this supper is communion

With Jesus and with those who follow Him:
His body nourishes our bodies and
We all are made one body by this meal.
We call it mystery, a sacrament,

Remembering His body and His blood
Poured out and broken for us, as the priests
In Moses' time would sacrifice a lamb
Atoning for the sins of Israel.

Night[42]

They tried to pray with Him, but fell asleep.
And in a darkened garden soldiers came;
Yes, Judas led them, showed them which was Jesus.
The soldiers took Him to be quartered, questioned.

While Peter waited by the prison, some
Asked if he followed Jesus. "No," he said.
And Jesus looked toward him and prayed for him.
Then Peter ran and hid with all the rest.

The priests interrogated Jesus, but
He stood in silence. They delivered Him
To waiting Romans with their spears and laws.

---

[42] Luke 22.

Betrayal

We say there are two images of how
A man betrays his lord within this story.
The first is Judas, who betrays for money,
And from a long resentment of his Lord.

And Judas, though he wishes he had not
Betrayed when all is done, does not repent
And dies in blank despair. But Peter, who
Betrayed his Lord as well, does so from fear,

And after his betrayal, does repent.
This second type takes refuge in God's mercy—
His every movement toward us is of love.

Friday[43]

The Roman governor was weary with
The Jewish people's cries of "Crucify!"
That was the punishment for criminals,
And Jesus didn't seem to him that kind.

But "Crucify!" they called so loud that he
Allowed them to take Jesus, beat Him, force
Their Christ to carry beams up to a hill.
And there the soldiers nailed Him to a cross.

Dark,
      Dark,
            Dark.

---

[43] Luke 23.

The Tree of the Cross

So many trees have weaved their branches with
Our story: first the tree within the garden,
Which our first parents ate from and so fell.
And then the tree that Christ Himself compared

To our own lives: He is the living trunk
In which we may be grafted and so bear
The fruit of faithful living. But what tree
Now lifts within His story? See the cross,

Its stark and budless trunk, its two dread limbs
On which the shaking limbs of criminals
Are stretched to waste and die. What good could gild
The surface of the lifeless crucifix?

Extreme Humility

We say that Jesus suffered all he did—
The beating, mocking, weight of wood, the nails
That pierced his hands and feet—all this he chose
For love of humankind. He bowed beneath

Each type of scorn and cruelty men can make,
Was humbled lower than the poorest thief.
He took the human world upon Himself
And knew the pain we know, was lonely and

Afraid as we can be. Identified
With every kind of pain, with every shame,
He showed the way of God: humility.

Dark[44]

The thief beside Him asks to be remembered.
Dark.
The people down below Him mock his words.
Dark.

His mother weeps. Beside her John is silent.
Dark.
Christ thirsts; He spits; He shudders; He cries out.
Dark.

"*I Am*, forgive them, for they do not know."
Dark.
"O why have You forsaken me, my God?"
Dark.

He whispers, "It is finished."

———

———

[44] Luke 23.

Forsaken

Was Jesus right when He cried from the cross
"My God you have forsaken me"? These words
Were spoken by a prophet long ago.
And Jesus placed Himself into the role

Of prophet, then, of crying out for all
Who felt themselves abandoned by *I am.*
But being God, He was not left alone.
As Son of God, He kept His nature still

As one eternally Divine, and—in
A mystery—He also suffered death
As one fully possessing human nature.

Saturday[45]

Within a tomb they laid him, my Redeemer.
——

Through tears the faithful women gathered spices.
——

A patron, Joseph, paid to have him buried.
——

The male disciples huddled in the dark.
——

And Judas, full of anguish, hung himself.
——

---

[45] Luke 23.

Broken

So much was broken when His body broke:
The old association of the gods
As distant, mocking beings to be feared;
The thought that pride and riches prove one's worth;

The very notion that a criminal
Is one to mock; that disability
And pain are somehow punishments for sin.
For now we say that God Himself was poor,

And torn, and crucified, and killed. His eyes
Were blank with common death. His side was pierced
To ratify all this—His fluids slid
Down from His wounds to wet the fruitless earth.

Silence[46]

That Saturday there was a silence in
All Israel—as if the voice of God
Had never spoken, could not ever speak.
The tomb of Jesus sat like other tombs,

A row of guards in front of it for fear
Disciples would attempt to steal His body.
The priests were anxious they'd not done enough
To stop this preacher sooner. And within

The tomb His body lay, as you and I
Will lie someday—just dead in humid air.

---

[46] Luke 23.

Dead

We say that He was truly dead—not some
Mistake of Roman medicine, not sleep
That seemed to be, but was not death. Real death
That you and I will die took Jesus, too.

Whatever death is—body left by soul—
He did experience. From Friday to
The night of Saturday, He lay entombed
And would have lain, decayed, and crumbled back

To dust, if not for something unexpected . . .

Empty[47]

The women who had followed Jesus came
On Sunday morning while it still was dark
To treat His corpse with myrrh, as custom said
Was right, as women have adorned the dead

For all of time: a little loveliness
To honor one more human gone to death.
But when the women found the tomb, they saw
The guards had fled. The open tomb now gaped

As if it had been hollowed out. Two angels
In shining robes appeared and asked: "Do you
Seek Life among the dead? He is not here,
For Christ is risen, just as He once said."

---

[47] Luke 24.

Harrowing

We say that when Christ's body was still dead
His soul down in the place of all the dead
Was active in a way not seen before.
His spirit preached to spirits down in Hell,

Undid the chains that bound them in their place
And led that host of captives back to light.
The enemies that barred his way were crushed—
The tempter, thinking that he'd won through death

Saw Life instead within the deepest hell,
And death now working backward—bearing fruit
As if dry sticks flared lush with spring again.

A Garden, again[48]

The women found Him in the garden walking,
The Man who'd been their friend, but somehow
    changed,
As if He'd passed from darkness into day
That could not now be dimmed by any night.

"Go now," He told them, "tell those who hide
In darkened rooms that I am risen—go
And tell them I am coming to them now."
When Peter, James, and John were told the news

By Mary and the other women, John
And Peter sprinted to the open tomb
To see for themselves that it was truly empty.

---

[48] Luke 24, John 20.

Evangelists

We say that in the garden God made first
A woman sinned and introduced that sin
To man who stood there with her. But in this,
The second garden next to Jesus' tomb,

A great reversal happened, for the women
Heard from the angel, then from Christ Himself,
The greatest news, that Christ is risen, and
They brought that news to men, who still were
        hiding.

"Cast off your ancient condemnation!" we
Now cry to all who sit in sin and fear,
"The women have become evangelists
Who speak salvation to the world of men!"

Commission[49]

And Jesus came, appeared to all the people
Who'd followed Him, and more. The news spread
    wide.
Though many doubted, those who did believe
Became evangelists. He sent them out:

"Now go and make disciples of the world,
And baptize them, invoking as you do
The Father, Son, and Spirit." Jesus lived
And talked and ate with them for forty days,

And then, atop a mountain, He ascended
Up—out—beyond their sight—leaving a promise:
"The Holy Spirit will be sent to you."

---

[49] Mark 16, Acts 1.

Resurrection

We say when Jesus rose he conquered death.
For though He was a man and thus could die,
He was divine, and death could not last long
Within His presence: He had drawn all things

From nothingness to being by His word
In the beginning: how could little death
Not wither at the power of His nature?
In rising from the dead, He showed that He

Is truly God and that humanity
Is capable of rising from the dead
If it unites with God's own nature now.

The Wind[50]

While gathered feasting in Jerusalem,
Disciples, men and women, heard a noise
Like wind, and down on each a light like flame
Descended. Then their languages were changed,

And they proclaimed the news of Jesus in
The tongues of many peoples: Jews and Greeks
And Africans and Persians and a host
Of all the tongues that humans speak on earth.

Then foreigners from every land passed on
The news throughout Jerusalem: "They speak
In every language dear to us of Christ!"
And many new believers joined their ranks.

---

[50] Acts 2.

Pentecost

We say that at this feast of Pentecost
The gathered followers of Jesus were
Indwelled by God's own Spirit in a new
And lasting way. The holy flames that fell

Upon their head were evidence that God
Had come to dwell within their midst, within
Their very spirits, and to give them gifts
Of faith and hope and love and power to

Begin to heal as Jesus healed, to preach
To all the human world, not just the Jews,
And power to create a Church in which
The ailing human spirit could be healed.

Churches[51]

Now those who had been called to go and preach
And baptize: Peter, James, and John, and all
The rest (excepting Judas) ventured out
To speak of Christ and found communities

That fed the hungry, clothed the poor, and taught
The doctrines Jesus gave them to the world.
They ran afoul of priests and governors
And kings who would condemn them to be killed,

But Christianity—the faith they taught—
Kept spreading, turning upside down the world.

---

[51] Acts 2–28.

Gospels and Epistles

Some followers of Jesus—Matthew, Mark,
And John—wrote stories of the life of Christ:
How He was born and preached and healed and died
To save the ailing world from sin and death,

Then resurrected. Others—Peter, James,
And Paul—wrote letters to the churches spread
Across the world, encouraging the Christians
In faithful living, right belief, and love.

These stories and these letters are held dear
By Christians to this day: we call them scripture.

Scripture

We say that scripture is the word of God,
Both Gospels and Epistles, younger heirs
To elder Law and Prophets—all are holy,
For they are God's communication to

All humans—not just Jews, or males, or kings—
But all who have been made in God's own image.
For God inspired and spoke through human words
And dignifies our speech with His own truth.

We say that words, though liable to err
Can be imbued with truth, and echo with
Commandments, doctrines, stories, all divine.

Memory

Recall the heroes now, before the end:
Of Abraham and Jacob, Rachel, Leah,
And of their son, the righteous Joseph who
Rejected tempting words and built a way

For Israel to live beyond their lack,
Of Moses who delivered Israel
Back home—of all these heroes we have sung,
And of the greatest hero: Jesus, Son

Of God, and of his Mother, Mary, and
His earthly father, Joseph, who returned
To Egypt in a rhyme of history,
And finally Christ's followers, now saints.

Revelation[52]

When Christ's disciples had passed into death,
And one remained—apostle John (and he
Was exiled on an island), then the Word
Of God came back to him, as it had done

To prophets since the dawn of history,
Revealed to him what would take place when time
Was at an end: when Jesus will return
To raise all who have died and to judge the world.

We say, "Come quickly, Lord," and also say:
"Be watchful, soul, the King of glory nears."

---

[52] Revelation 1–22.

The Last Judgment

We say that just as Christ rose from the dead,
One day all will be raised—all will be judged
According to their love. God will not force
Those who have set their will against His own

To live united with Himself. We say
Hell is that place for those who will reject
God's offer of Himself: both men and angels
Can enter into it, but will not find

Fulfillment there. We cannot say or know
Who will reject Him in the end—we say:
Judge no one else; instead, look to yourself.

A New Earth

No, all will not depart into the dark.
For some, the saints, those baptized into Christ,
Communing with Him in His holy meal,
Will find a new uniting with Him there

On worlds transfigured, time and sadness ceased,
Where love of God in all makes all things sweet.
Our natures rooted into His will be
Transformed, participating in His life,

And bloom into a fruit we cannot guess.
We say these words, but know that God is past
All languages. He meets us in the realm
Of speech—and can redeem our meanings still.

Epilogue: What Must I Do?

A man once asked Saint Paul: "What must I do
To gain salvation?" And the Saint replied,
"Believe in Jesus Christ, and you'll be saved;
Be baptized; bring your family, your whole

Conception of community and time,
And plunge within the sacramental stream."
Salvation is a moment and a life,
A stark, dramatic turning and a slow,

Deep nourishment and growth. O River deep,
O precious Springtime of the riven earth,
What must we do but turn and rest in You?

Further Reading

Those looking to learn more about the Christian faith would do well to read those books of the Bible that are referenced in the notes to these poems, most importantly the books of Genesis, Exodus, Luke, and Acts.

Two creeds from the early Christian era, the Apostles' Creed and the Nicene Creed, are good summations of Christian doctrine, and have been important for the last two millennia in summing up what Christians believe. These creeds have been reproduced below.

Finally, out of the many books of theology and apologetics that have been written over the centuries, several may be of particular help to those seeking to know more about the Christian faith.

1) *On the Incarnation*, by St Athanasius of Alexandria. This book, written by a 4th century African bishop, explains who Christ is and why his incarnation, death, and resurrection are so central to human history.

2) *Mere Christianity*, by C.S. Lewis. Lewis is famous for his clear and winsome explanation of Christian ethics

and theology. A great companion piece to his
Chronicles of Narnia novels.

3) *The Christian Tradition: A History of the Development
of Doctrine*, by Jaroslav Pelikan. Pelikan's multi-volume
history is a comprehensive explanation of how
Christian doctrine developed from the New
Testament through the 20th century. Not for the
casual reader.

Two Ancient Christian Creeds

The Apostles' Creed

I believe in God, the Father almighty, Creator of
heaven and earth, and in Jesus Christ, his only Son,
our Lord, who was conceived by the Holy Spirit, born
of the Virgin Mary, suffered under Pontius Pilate, was
crucified, died and was buried; he descended into
hell; on the third day he rose again from the dead; he
ascended into heaven, and is seated at the right hand
of God the Father almighty; from there he will come
to judge the living and the dead.

I believe in the Holy Spirit, the holy catholic Church,
the communion of saints, the forgiveness of sins, the
resurrection of the body, and life everlasting.

Amen.

The Nicene Creed

We believe in one God, the Father Almighty, Maker
of heaven and earth, and of all things visible and
invisible;

And in one Lord Jesus Christ, the Son of God, the Only-begotten, Begotten of the Father before all ages, Light of Light, Very God of Very God, Begotten, not made; of one essence with the Father; by Whom all things were made:

Who for us men and for our salvation came down from heaven, and was incarnate of the Holy Spirit and the Virgin Mary, and was made man; And was crucified also for us under Pontius Pilate, and suffered and was buried; And the third day He rose again, according to the Scriptures; And ascended into heaven, and sits at the right hand of the Father; And He shall come again with glory to judge the living and the dead, Whose kingdom shall have no end.

And we believe in the Holy Spirit, the Lord, and Giver of Life, Who proceeds from the Father, Who with the Father and the Son together is worshipped and glorified, Who spoke by the Prophets;

And we believe in one, holy, catholic, and apostolic Church. We acknowledge one Baptism for the remission of sins. We look for the Resurrection of the dead, And the Life of the age to come. Amen.